DIM LIGHT

LIGHT

BONITA RENEA

PALMETTO
PUBLISHING
Charleston, SC
www.PalmettoPublishing.com

Copyright © 2024 by Bonita Renea

All rights reserved

No portion of this book may be reproduced, stored in a retrieval system, or transmitted in any form by any means–electronic, mechanical, photocopy, recording, or other–except for brief quotations in printed reviews, without prior permission of the author.

Paperback ISBN: 9798822962446

Contents

A Note from the Author vii
Introduction ix
Era One: A 9-Year-Old's Heartbreak 1
Era Two: Falling Through It 14
Era Three: When a Flower Blooms 52
A Whole Lot of Nothing About Something 62

A Note from the Author

The Broken Child, The Healing Woman!

The beauty of not knowing everything **is that you do not know everything.** There is always room to learn. This makes life's journey more fulfilling. To start, sharing such intimate, raw truths about yourself is hard. What I have found to be true is that even hard things become beautiful. This book is my baby. I started writing in 2018, and then life happened. The start never matters, only the finish. This book is my journey of recognizing that we all walk our paths while healing, but they are ours.

I hope this book helps you on your journey to healing. May there be more love and light for each of you.

Introduction

My life, in words, travels through some of my most pivotal moments. Each of these moments reflects the space I was in then. I am not proud of every moment, but every moment is mine. I OWN it. It belongs to me. I wanted to use the things that have happened in my life to show that when we own who we are, hold ourselves accountable, and face the things that scare us most, we can create a beautiful life we love. I have given myself grace and room to grow. I hope this translates and we can all fly together.

All my love, Bonita

ERA ONE

A 9-Year-Old's Heartbreak

A broken heart is a metaphor for the intense emotional stress or pain one feels when experiencing great and deep longing. The concept is cross-cultural and often concerns unreciprocated or lost love.

Heartbreaks started at an early age for me. I was repeatedly getting my heart broken by the same man—my dad. The man who was supposed to protect me had become the reason I knew what pain felt like. It started when I was six.

My Dad
I looked at my dad as if he were not human. To me, he was the absolute best man. I also looked at him as a shadow man. His spirit often felt like a shadow that hid behind closed doors, and his darkness daunted where no one could see. Therefore, while he was my Superhero, he also existed as a man in the shadows.

My Mom
I never felt more at peace and loved than when I was with both of my parents, especially my mother. She was so soft and gentle. The way she loved me was so pure and unconditional. It transcended. She had this way of pulling you in with her laugh. In our house, we had each other. She needed me to cry on, and I needed to be there for her. There would be moments when I would just lay on her, and she would rub my head or

back. Sometimes, it seemed like I was holding her. We had an unbreakable bond, and I felt it. Her love saw me.

Our Shadows

We initially started as a church-going family. My dad sang duets with our Pastor's first lady. I enjoyed it when we attended church as a family and participated heavily in church. However, the shadow man lived a lie, so we, in turn, lived a lie. See, the thing about a lie is that you can only hold on to it for so long before it shows its face. Therefore, what started as our family together turned into just my mother and me. I spent my entire childhood pretending, so pretending became my reality.

I cannot speak to early childhood moments that I remember being consistently happy. The pretending continued, so I never fully came to terms with the fact that my actual reality consisted of my dad being abusive to my mother and me. He only physically abused my mother; nevertheless, he mentally and emotionally abused us both. I also could not connect this to abuse at the time because I was so young.

What I did know was that it did not feel right, but I assumed that this was just how things were. Things go this way. No one gives you a play-by-play on what abuse looks or feels like, especially in the early 90's. It can wrap you up unintentionally. I began to exist as a kid. My life had one purpose. I was only here to protect my mother from my father. He abused my mother for most of my early childhood. It was on every level. Verbal, physical, mental and emotional. He cheated, had me around other women, lied, gambled all of my mother's money away, made my cousin Chasiti and I sit in the car while he tormented my mother, and the list goes on.

*Let's quickly unpack emotional trauma and generational curses. *

My dad would beat my mother, but this was a learned behavior. He learned a trauma that he, in turn, passed on to me—his child. Black families are known to pass over generational trauma versus generational wealth, and it is not entirely our fault. The behaviors and cycles are learned because of adaptation. Environment and Proximity are critical factors in a child's upbringing. We must unpack our childhood traumas, to not unload these things onto our children and spouses. My dad did not. He never thought he had a problem, but he did.

Two things:
1) Accountability
2) Do the work

In life, you must hold yourself accountable and then do the necessary work to be a better human. None of us are perfect, and we all have shortcomings. Taking ownership of your choices and actions begins to help you heal because no one can weaponize the flaws you own. When you take responsibility for who you are and want to be, you understand it means accepting all the good and bad parts. You do not deny any part that comes with you. That is when you genuinely start to dive into your true self. Doing the work is all good until it is not because there will be moments when you want to give up. However, you cannot give up. Giving up and not pushing yourself is one of the hardest lessons to learn, yet one of the easiest things to do. It is so easy to remain stagnant and not grow. However, if you do not change, no growth occurs.

A Shift

I just knew that after the last time my dad physically abused my mother, I could help him stop. Imagine being a nine-year-old trying to stop a grown man from abuse. We had been staying with my Aunt Renea for a couple of months because it seemed this time my mother could no longer continue life with my dad. She decided for the first time in 17 years to walk away from her abusive husband. Walking away came at a cost: her life. My dad killed her on April 10th, 1996, because she chose herself and her child this time. He told me he would kill her, although he did not say it directly. He alluded to the fact he planned to take my mother's life.

Hollow

I was headed to a sleepover at my cousin Sweetie's house. It was no different from any other sleepover that we always had. Little did I know how much my life would change. Before heading to the sleepover, I talked to my dad. I was slightly annoyed talking to him because I was ready to go. We were on Spring Break, and I wanted to go with my cousins. While on this call, my dad told me, "Hey baby girl, you know I love you, right?" I replied very exhaustedly, "Yes, Daddy, I know." The next thing he said to me did not make sense then because I was ready to go to the sleepover. I heard what he was saying, but I was not listening. "You are going to see me on the news tomorrow, ok, but no matter what anyone tells you, I love you." I said, "Ok." Being that I was a kid, while I knew what the shadow man did at home, murder never crossed my mind.

My cousin Sweetie woke up Chasiti and me. She told us we were getting ready to be picked up and said it sounded like my mama. It was early that morning, and I wondered why my mama was coming to get us so early. I wanted to stay longer or an additional night. I could not fathom for a moment the turn my life was about to take. Chasiti and I got together and waited for my mama to get there, but my mama did not walk through the door.

My Aunts Bonita and Renea walked in, which was oddly surprising. My Aunt Bonita lived in Columbia, South Carolina, so seeing her was a bit of a shock to me.

Although I was shocked, I was also happy to see her. At that time in my life, she was strangely foreign to me. She was one of the most magical people I knew and lived far away. I did not recognize or understand it yet, but she enamored me. I still did not acknowledge that something was wrong because everything at that moment felt okay.

Then I looked at my Aunt Renea's face, which told a melancholy story. Something about the moment did not feel safe. It was such an eerie feeling. As Chasiti and I were getting ready to walk out the door, my aunt said, "Bonita, sit down for a moment; we want to talk to you about something."

I began to breathe heavily and snapped out of kid mode. It was such an awkward feeling that had grabbed hold of me. My Aunt Renea said to me with as much strength as she had. "There's been an accident." Every possible scenario began to play in my head. I have always had the gift of feeling. Things for me have always translated on a much deeper spiritual level. In the moment before I found out my mother had been killed, I unknowingly began to wilt. I felt something had gone wrong.

"What kind of accident"? I asked. My Aunt Bonita looked at me and said, "There's been an accident with your mom." I could feel the tears forming in my eyes; however, for some reason, I did not want the tears to fall because tears meant something terrible happened. My gut knew something wrong had occurred, but I was not ready to face this truth.

"Is she ok"? I asked with a cracking voice, and many held back tears. My Aunt Bonita replied calmly but with the presence of pain, "She's resting," she said. "Resting where"? Was my next question because I wanted to see her, "She's resting in her resting place." I started to cry out loudly. I did not realize how loud my cry was. For so long, my emotions were silenced. I could not cry aloud or be upset about things that hurt me. I was never allowed to talk about the daily trauma my mother, and I endured at the hands of my father. This personal, necessary cry shattered my heart. I was a nine-year-old little girl who had just lost both of her parents, and suddenly, everything went pitch black.

Quiet

There were moments after my mom died when I was confused, and then there were moments when I was quiet. I am not usually quiet; I am very talkative and always have been, but this time, **I DID NOT HAVE ANYTHING TO SAY**. I did not want to talk to anyone, and even though I was sad, I did not feel like dealing with people. I already felt miserable.

Sometimes, when people asked me how I felt, I would say, "I don't know," but most times, I would say, "I'm ok."

The reality of this was I was never ok. I was hurting. Never in my wildest dreams did I imagine my mother and father not being here. I no longer knew who I was anymore. I felt abandoned and ultimately forgotten. There was a mediocre moment when I did not know how my life would turn out. Remember, I had gotten good at pretending from the shadow man. He taught me how to lie, and so did my mom. While my mother's scenario stemmed from fear, it still happened. I learned how to pretend and lie, which is who I became.

Here, we must reflect on what was happening. I was a nine-year-old child who had just lost her mom to murder by her father. I was in total shock and denial.

There are seven stages of grief:
1) Shock and denial
2) Pain and Guilt
3) Anger and Bargaining
4) Depression
5) The upward tum
6) Reconstruction and working through
7) Acceptance and Hope.

I do not know if anyone around me recognized it, but I did not come out of stage one for a while. There were so many moving parts to my situation. Who was I going to live with? Would I be there permanently? Would my dad's family have access to me? Unbelievably, my nine-year-old brain was asking every single possible question. I was so uninterested in being a kid. I did not have the time to do that. I had to figure out (in my nine-year-old mind) where I would live.

I made the decision to live with my Aunt Renea. That is where I wanted to be. Growing up, she knew me best; she was all I knew. If we were not living with them, they were living with us.

Surprisingly, I was told I would be living with my godparents. However, before I dig into that part of my life, I have to be clear on how much everything changed instantly for me. Including having to testify against my dad. The conversation he had with me the evening before he murdered my mother was going to be used as evidence for our prosecution team.

While hard was an understatement, so was easy. I had to tell the truth and defend my mother. All of this was indeed a whirlwind. Usually, we lied. We lied about what my father did to us, about our home's destructive environment, about my mother's bruises and mostly everything. My mama told me, "Don't ever tell anyone what happens here, especially Renea." I never told the truth until I did not have a choice.

The court proceedings drained me. I tried to act as if they did not because I wanted to be there. If I seemed bothered, they may not let me go. I was not allowed to view my mother's body when she initially died; however, I wanted to. I wanted to see her because I wanted to touch her, feel her. I did not get that chance, so I had to be in that courtroom for her. Initially, I was nervous about facing my father, but I looked him right in the eyes and testified. My heart, yet again, had been broken.

I began to adapt to being hurt. It was customary for me. The trial ended, and my father was found guilty and sentenced to life in prison. I was allowed to talk to him briefly before they took him away. I asked him, eye-to-eye, "Daddy, why did you do this"? He had no answer for me. I cried the hardest that day, the hardest I had probably cried in my life. I could not stop. I tried to stop, I did, but the tears continued to flow. After the trial, we ate at Red Lobster, and I still cried. My Aunt Renea looked at me and said, "Ok, Bonita, that's enough", stop all that crying."

My Aunt Renea loves me and would do anything for me, including laying down her life for mine. She is one of my shero's and has loved me in my lowest moments. However, at that moment, my moment to mourn was taken from me. I was not crying so hard for my dad. I was crying excessively because I had officially lost both of my parents. The two people

I lived with my entire life until now. My mama was dead, and the shadow man was just that, a shadow. They were both now gone forever.

I wish that who I am today could hold my nine-year-old self. I was so afraid, yet I knew life would continue at this very young age, whether I wanted it to or not.

A MOMENT TO UNPACK

I lost my parents and did not properly have a moment to process everything that happened to me. This translated to me that we could cry momentarily when things hurt, but after that, we must stop. We do not process things or heal through them. My aunt telling me to stop crying created another lifelong ripple effect of pretending. She did not know this then, nor did she understand it. She, too, had endured a loss, and not just any loss, her sister and best friend. She was also young, only 26. Now that I am an adult, I understand how to unpack these scenarios properly. I realize now that two things can be true at once.

She also taught me that life does not stop at tears. Regardless, we have to keep pushing through. We have to fight and advocate for ourselves, especially when we are pushing through pain. Crying is okay, but once we stop crying, we have to keep living.

The day of my father's trial changed me more than I understood then. It may have had an even more substantial impact on me than the day I found out my mother died. The reason for that is I never processed my mother's death initially. I was still very much in shock. I think one time I even thought, "Maybe she faked her death to get away from my dad." This saddened me because why would she leave me? It was not until I saw her in the casket for the first time that I realized it was true. She was gone. I touched her face to see if this was real because she looked like a doll sleeping. She was beautiful. Her hair was perfect like it had always been, but she was hard and cold. I had nowhere to go but to face the truth. She was dead, and she was never coming back.

Chaos

My Godparents love me dearly. They took me into their home and showed me what a two-parent home is supposed to look like. While all this was true, I still did not want to live with them. I wanted to live with my Aunt Renea. At no point in time, living with them did this change. I think I rebelled because I did not want to live there. I kept telling lies because that is what I was taught. The truth was not in me. I also loved them, but I did not trust them. I was a broken child with trust issues. All of this was new to me. I trusted the man who gave me life, and he killed the woman who gave me life. How does that work?

I look back now and wish I had treated them better during my time there, but I did not know how. I wanted them to give up on me and send me to live with my aunt, but they never did. I often told my Aunt Renea that I wanted to come and live with her. I wondered how long it would take before this happened. I was beginning to resent everyone. I really should have been in some therapy, but it was taboo at the time and never happened.

Black People get THERAPY. It is okay. I needed it, and it made life a little easier. Therapy is a staple in healing. You still have to do inner work to understand who you are and how to improve; however, it is a tool.

At this point, I was beginning to go through the second and third phases of grief.

*Pain and Guilt.
*Anger and Bargaining.

I started a play-by-play about what I could have done to save my parents. Maybe I could have said more; perhaps I should have spoken up. Maybe I could have told the multiple women my dad cheated with that he had a family. Maybe turned into, I SHOULD HAVE. I should have killed my dad before he killed my mom. I should have called the police more than the one time I did.

Calling the police on my dad was one of the hardest things I think I ever did; however, nobody deserved my loyalty more than my mother. This would be his last time hurting her before I killed him. It had gotten to that point for me. I could no longer take the abuse of my mother.

One day after he finished beating her, I finally gained the courage to call the police. I felt so horrible afterward that as he was packing his belongings to leave by a police escort, I tried to hug him, and he pushed me to the side.

This one particular moment also caused me to act a certain way in life as it pertained to men and their abuse towards me. We will gravitate to that a little later, but it was a pivotal moment in how my life would look with men who mirrored my father. All these things played in my mind as I went through stages of grief; what I was not prepared for was what happened next.

Within six or seven months of living with my Godparents, they told me I would live with my aunt. At this point, I got excited. However, I quickly became befuddled after I learned it would be my Aunt Bonita, not Renea. ***I DID NOT WANT TO.***

I was familiar with my Aunt Bonita (Aunt Boot). I knew who she was, but I did not know her. As I stated earlier, she was like a foreign creature to me, extremely mystique.

Now, in my 9-year-old brain, I created a plan. I would do ridiculous things until she let me stay with Aunt Renea. This goes to show how much I knew about Bonita Clemons. I had no clue at the time that she would be everything I needed and more.

Before I left my Godparents to stay with my Aunt Bonita, they sat me down and asked me if I wanted to go and if I was sure.

I told them, "Yes." This was my way out. The last conversation with my Godparents was somewhat hurtful. I did not understand many things as a kid, and I think being a kid may have gotten lost in translation somewhere along the way. This was a different time in life.

Now that I am an adult, I can truly understand all parties involved and perspectives. It was indeed a fight for my custody and almost a family divided on where I would stay. I can now see everyone's frustration and emotions that affected how I would live the rest of my life. While I was hurt, I did not intend to go back. However, I was willing to be chaotic until I returned with my Aunt Renea.

The day I left my Godparents' house was one of the first days in a long time that I felt like life might be okay. I never thought it would be good, but okay worked just fine.

Healing Points

1) *Allow children to be children.*

Allow children to exist in a space of love and understanding. Guide and teach them. Allow them to be expressive, and discipline them in a way they understand. Although sometimes parenting can be frustrating, kids are just little people with big feelings and energy. I am new to parenthood, but I am enjoying the journey of learning. We are not always correct as parents. Sometimes, our children are the teachers, and we are the students. Do not be afraid to let those moments happen.

2) *Keep your children's environment free of toxic stress.*

The only thing children should have to worry about is absolutely nothing. Kids do not ask to be here. As parents, our job is to protect and give them love throughout their lives. Putting stress on your children, especially at a young age, creates open wounds. One day, they will grow up. You do not want them to be caged by these things. Give them a fair shot at creating their own lives.

3) *DO NOT DUMP YOUR TRAUMA ONTO YOUR CHILDREN.*

We must, as a community of people, take the necessary steps to deal with our trauma. Everyone has a story, but you are also the author. Trauma dumping onto your kids creates their trauma, which they can potentially drop onto their kids. We are breaking generational curses and moving towards trauma freedom.

4) *Grief is a process.*

*It never ends. Life, of course, goes on, but you still grieve. Trust your process and allow it to happen.

The only absolute thing we know is that we are going to die.

Death is inevitable. We still must understand and know that it is ok to grieve. Do not let anyone rush your process or make you feel you should move on. It does not work that way. Again, trust your process. We all grieve differently. If you feel something in grief, feel it. Allow it to happen. The process is a journey you will endure for the remainder of your life. Be patient with yourself on this path. *

5) Abuse is more than physical. It starts with your mind and then emotions. Physical comes last.

*If you are in an abusive relationship, GET OUT. If someone says, "They will kill you," they will. They are not using scare tactics; they are speaking from an authentic place that is scary. Although hard to understand, some people do exist in that energy. Do not ignore the signs and protect yourself. If you have children, think of them as well. Navigating this world without your parents is gut-wrenching, especially for a child. *

6) Trust your Gut

When something is shit, it stinks. You know what feels right and what does not. Trust your gut because it is also a part of your guide. It is your spirit telling you, "This ain't it."

7) Give yourself grace.

Don't be so hard on yourself in your healing journey. You deserve the grace you give to others. Honor and love yourself. It is an integral part of the journey. You owe it to you to be here for you. It does not matter if the moment is less appealing or accessible. Giving yourself grace allows you to give grace to others.

ERA TWO

Falling Through It

Learning who I was and growing into myself played a massive part in this era of my life. I was such a young woman full of life, but I also carried a lot of pain with me, and it exuded.

B SQUARED

I am humored by how clueless I was about the woman Bonita Clemons is. I could not have fathomed that she was exactly who I needed to shape the new trajectory of my life. She taught me self-love, responsibility, to be independent, and to love the skin that I am in and own it. The most important thing she taught me was how to begin healing. She prepared me to take care of myself if something happened to her. She gave me all the tools to be a successful young black woman.

    However, at that time, I was young and dumb. I wanted to do things my way. As previously stated, my main objective was to live with my Aunt Renea. I knew my Aunt Bonita loved me, but I still did not know her. She lived in Columbia, SC. At the time, as a kid, that seemed so far away to me, slightly an unrealistic place.

    On my first day living with my aunt, she told me straight to the point.
1) Wake yourself up each morning for school.
2) Wash and dry your clothes.
3) You will learn how to cook for yourself

Of course, I said, "I don't know how," and she responded, "I know, but I'm going to teach you," and she did. I was a latchkey kid. My aunt has always been the busiest person I know, and she still is to this day. She always kept her hands in many different pots, which is also one of the things I learned from her.

I moved to Columbia with her in the 4th grade. I attended an all-black Christian school, which was my first experience at an all-black school. After learning about my aunt, it made sense for me to be there.

I would like to think that my aunt could sense my immense sadness, so we moved back to Anderson, SC. I now understand it was divine timing.

In my young brain, my plan was working. I was getting closer and closer to living with my Aunt Renea. Just months before we moved, I decided I would run away. I did not know where I was running to, but I did not want to live with my Aunt Bonita.

I packed some clothes, went outside, and began to try to hitchhike a ride. I was yearning for some attention. I needed that from my aunt. I could not connect to her internal pain; while I did not feel like a kid, I was still very much a kid. I was too young to recognize the magnitude of what she did for me. She took me in at 31 with no biological children of her own. She was single, successful, a college graduate, intelligent, and driven, and she had just lost her sister to murder, also.

Now that I am in my mid-30s, I realize how young she was. If anyone was owed a better version of me, it was her. I honestly did not want to be good to anyone. The people I loved the most were gone, and my Aunt Renea had still not gotten me. I was sick of everyone in my life. I missed my mama. I wanted her back so badly that it hurt. I yearned for her; no one would rest since I could not have her. I would continue to rebel.

My brain knew precisely right and wrong, but I had to stay in the shadows before I could live in the light. Just like the shadow man had taught me to do. Now that I am an adult who has done the necessary work and unpacked my traumas, I have learned children's core behaviors and patterns are based on ages 0–7 years. This is the foundation of a child's traits and nature. Children who grow up in chaotic environments usually carry those characteristics throughout childhood. Children who experience trauma look at the world through much different lenses than those who do not.

They experience an unending pain and carry it. One of my core traumas was lying. Although I knew it was wrong, it was the foundation of my childhood. I also did not think anyone around me was honest or truthful. I felt things were being hidden from me. I know I was a kid, but I never felt that way because, in my mind, *"Kids had parents."* I did not understand why I could not live with my Aunt Renea. I asked the question often because it was always on my mind.

Once we finally moved back to Anderson, SC, I was around my Aunt Renea more, and it felt better because she was there. I still lived with my Aunt Bonita, but my Aunt Renea was close to my life. I began growing up. Ten turned to fifteen quickly. My life was starting to normalize. Things were going exactly as I had planned, and I was getting closer and closer to living with my Aunt Renea.

This next small part gives a little insight into my dad's family. After I lost my parents, I did not hear from my dad's family again. I never talked to them, even though I wanted to. I felt slightly abandoned by them. I felt like they were mad at me for testifying against my dad. That also confused me and did not make sense, but it became a reality I faced head-on. I still, however, believed that they loved me and missed me. I stayed hopeful because I did love them, too.

The Reunion

My dad had five other children, two boys and three girls, all older than me. I always knew my oldest brother, who lived with us briefly. He was one of my favorite people in the world. We just clicked—we always did.

Over two years, from six to eight years old, I learned about my sisters and met them. My oldest sister even came and stayed with us for a little while. Having siblings was always the one thing I adored. I grew up as an only child most of my life, but I always wanted siblings. I had met all my siblings except one.

I was an athlete, and I played basketball. One day, at one of my games, I saw a boy who looked exactly like my dad sitting in the stands. It began to puzzle me because they looked identical. For some strange reason, I immediately felt connected to this stranger. I kept watching him, and he kept smiling at me. When the game was over, I walked up to him. For all I knew, he could have been a kidnapper or anything, but I wanted to know who he was. I asked him right away, "Do you know me?" He replied, "Yes, little sister."

My mouth dropped. I asked him if he was my brother and I said his name. He said, "Yes, I am, and we have the same dad." We hugged, and he told me his life was complete because he had met me. We talked for a second, and he smiled a lot. He took my number and told me he would call me. I was so happy about meeting him.

The next day, he killed himself. I was not prepared to grieve for someone that I did not know, but I did. I wanted to pay my brother his respect and go to his funeral. My brother, sisters, and I also attended a private viewing where my dad was allowed. I remember walking up to his casket and him looking so much like my dad that it scared me.

My dad walked in, and my heart dropped for a moment. This was my first time seeing him since I was nine. Six years had passed without me hearing one word from my father. I had so many mixed emotions at this point. I remember cracking a joke saying, "Dang daddy, why you got them bifocals on"? He laughed and said, "Well, they don't really give you the best choices where I am." We laughed, and he looked at me. I looked back.

We ended up leaving, and they took me back to school. I was told they would come and pick me back up for the funeral later that day. I waited for about two hours, and even though I knew what time the funeral started, I still waited. No one ever showed up. I never realized how much them leaving me, alienated me. I never heard a word or explanation from my grandmother (dad's mom); they never returned. That day changed me a little more. It made me a little more afraid to open myself up. Moreover, it made me realize that my dad's family did not want me there. At least, that is how I felt, and that hurt me in a way I could not process.

Starting Over

The longer we stayed in Anderson, SC, the more it seemed my aunt's rose petals were falling. My aunt is enormously energetic; she needed to return to Columbia, SC, to thrive. I did not understand it then, but moving was our best decision. My aunt needed to spread her wings again, and it was time for me to fly. I needed the change.

As I got older, I continued to rebel. I did not feel seen or heard. I DID NOT want to move. I had just started to get a rhythm to my life. I completed my first year of high school as a working honor student and athlete. This move did not make sense.

I decided not to talk to my aunt. I have always been a fighter. As young as 15, I knew you had to stand for something, and this move felt unjust. I wanted to stay with my Aunt Renea, so I decided not to talk to my Aunt Bonita for a while. I had to take a stand; meanwhile, she has not been wrong about a decision regarding me yet. She has always had my best interest at heart. She even made sure I got some therapy. Everything she has taught me has prepared me for who I am today. Her grace still enamors me, and I am amazed at her brilliance. I feel like she can do anything in the world.

Bonita and Renea saved my life. They showed me unconditional, unwavering love, even in my least deserving moments. I am honored to be their namesake. My mother knew something we did not by naming me after them. I have both of them inside of me, and I will forever cherish how they never let me fail, no matter what. The love of aunties is a staple in this world for healing.

In Pieces

This particular time of my life was one of the wildest times of unimaginable pain. Despite trying to learn, I had no clue who I was; the lessons came slowly. I kept acting as if I was happy, but I was not. I had so much to learn in this era, but a quick moment of transparency. (I had no desire to learn).

I had grown into a young woman, 18 years old and fresh to college. Strangely, I wanted so badly to fall in love. This came with a lot of failed attempts and disappointments. I always thought I put myself in a position to be taken seriously as a young woman. I thought the young men in my life understood that.

Nevertheless, how? How could the young men in my life understand me when I did not know or understand myself? It also seemed like I was having an identity crisis with who I was and who they wanted me to be. Failing at relationships happened a lot. I was searching for a fairytale, this happily ever after, yet no work on my end had been applied. Just thinking about it now makes me laugh, but it was not funny then. I wanted these serious relationships, yet I was still young and learning.

I must note that all the relationships I will write about describe an unhealed version of myself in a highly chaotic place. Most of these encounters happened when I was a kid, turning into a young adult. These are some of my unspoken truths.

Much of my life was centered on my relationships with men (Boys), a direct trickle effect of my life with my dad. He was not the only person who hurt me as a kid.

A long-distance relative molested me also. For a long time, I had this tainted image of myself. I felt like adults looked at me as (a fast young girl). I do not know if it was because of how the story was told initially, but I felt I did something wrong. I never intended to tell because I did not understand the magnitude of what had happened. I also felt like it was my fault. It was not. I wish to wrap my arms around my seven-year-old self and tell her that. ***The blood in the tub told my truth because I never would have.***

Remember, I lived in the shadows. The shadow man protected me every step of the way in the court proceedings, even when I had to testify against my predator.

Two years later, I did the same thing against my dad. My relationship with men was a long and scary journey—a very hurtful place to be. I did not recognize that I had any trauma or even really know what that meant.

18-Year-Old B

I started to realize what kind of guys I was attracted to and liked. It was not the good guys on paper. I wanted the thrill. I wanted the guy all the girls wanted—the most popular, the finest, the one who was fly. We did not need chemistry or a connection. As long as he looked good and was charismatic, I was his. This makes no sense now that I am in my 30s.

I am fresh to college and a little boy crazy. I am trying not to give off that vibe, but I am. While I was, boys also liked me, so I used that to my advantage. You had to put your plot out there in college, or a friend could snatch the person you wanted or liked right from you. Doing this also caused a slight discrepancy with a former friend.

College taught me a lot about men and their games, but of course, it would. We were all kids growing into young adults. I loved this one person in college, in particular. He meant a lot to me. He had a girlfriend unbeknownst to me initially.

Once I learned about her, I was too far gone and head over hills for him. He was the guy all the girls wanted, and I had him. Regardless of his girlfriend, in my mind, I was his girlfriend. We were together all day, every day.

Growth understands that I was not his girlfriend and he was not my boyfriend. He was a guy with a girlfriend and some women on the side, and I was one of them.

I also did not regard other women at this time in my life. It was all about what I wanted. I had no thought of other girls' feelings. I had an "every man for themselves mind frame." My ego and desire to always be number one drove me heavily. I now recognize that those were soft insecurities within myself, constantly feeling superior, but I was not the better choice then. Things that are meant for someone else will always be. You cannot make what is not meant for you belong to you. The Universe has a funny way of showing you exactly who you are and will be. There is room for all of us. When you know who you are, you exist in it. Tearing another person down to big yourself up says a lot about the person you are.

I remember one night with this person. We were vibing and kicking it like we always did. I asked him, "What do you love about the other girl?" He looked at me, puzzled that I asked because we usually did not talk about her. However, I wanted to know. I only wanted to know so that I could compete. He was still looking at me and charmingly said, "I'm here with you." Then, I asked with all my heart and soul, "Do you love me?" He looked at me with those dreamy eyes and said, "I have a lot of love for you."

This pissed me off and made me sad too. I spent every single day with this person. We were also very intimate, often. Every day, all day. What did he mean he did not love me? Nothing about what he said at that moment made sense to me.

*A moment to learn *

It did make sense. He told me he had a girlfriend, and even though it was not initially, he still told me. I chose to continue having sex with him, and I continued giving him all my free time knowing this.

So yes, he had the time to see me daily; he also had the time to have sex, but his emotional capacity was at its max. He had a girlfriend to whom his feelings and emotions belonged; I had no place there.

I blamed him for continuing to reach out and see me. I kept telling myself, "He's reaching out to me," but I never took accountability for my role. I kept responding, and I kept going back.

I continued dealing with him. In hindsight, I was getting what I deserved, even though his words and actions did not align. It was not his responsibility to protect me in any way, as we were not in a relationship. (Hard Truth)

I wanted us to be together so badly that I lied about being pregnant. Writing this now makes me cringe, but it is my truth. I went back to what I had always known: lying. The lie was a colossal flop; the same former friend called it out. It also did not work, and it made me look foolish. I did not even directly tell him; I told our friends.

Honestly, this may have been one of my most problematic moments. My desperation was so loud at this time. I wanted him to want me the way I wanted him. I should have realized that life only sometimes works this way. Admitting this embarrassed me, but it needed to happen. I was seeking validation from him, amongst other things, which he was unwilling to give me.

The signs were always right before me, but I ignored them. I felt I could somehow change his mind. There had to be a way. There were also numerous moments when he made decisions, and I was not his choice.

Whether I was or not did not matter because I was not what he wanted then. We have to remember that we, as women, hold the power.

Even though he was not a bad person, he was just **not my person**. I wanted to play a blame game: "Oh, you hurt me," and "You did this to me." While he may have hurt me, I hurt myself as well. All the answers to my questions were right in front of me.

He and I still communicated in life and remained friends. We both had to grow. Later in life, I also received apologies from this person, and I apologized, too. We were both young.

I also realized we were much better as friends anyway. It is also okay to befriend the opposite sex without the extra. You can like someone, and they like you, but you are still only meant to be friends.

The lesson is that what is meant for you will never pass you by. What is yours is yours. There will never be a moment when you must compete for what is yours because it was specifically designed for you. Sometimes, we are caught up in, "Well, I want that too," or "I thought that was mine." You will not have to think or question it when it is yours.

RED FLAGS THAT WILL SLAP YOU

I had boyfriends, but they were never serious enough to go anywhere. This part of my life also gets outrageous and dangerous.

Before we get into this, I want to be clear: writing this all down is still hard. It is hard because this was one of the absolute lowest points in my life. I did not know who I was. I was still a young girl searching and longing for a love that was not there.

I have always told my mother's story, but never my own. I was also embarrassed. I could not see my delusion as I was in the thick of it. I also never shared because I did not want to make anyone seem like a villain. Honestly, people can grow and change. Whether we know it or not, we may be a villain in someone else's story from their perspective. Nevertheless, **THIS IS MY TRUTH AND MY STORY TO TELL.** I own every part, even mine. It belongs to me. If I can help another person end cycles, I am living my life's purpose. I was in an abusive cycle but did not think so because my world was always pretending. I lived in the shadows for a long time. I am no longer afraid to exploit my truths so that no soul can use them against me.

The very first red flag came packaged neatly with a bow. My sunflower, my cousin Brittney, handed it to me. Before I met him, she warned me of some red flags she had known. I did not listen. I was a person who wanted what I wanted, no matter what it looked like.

I ran into him a couple of times, and this last time, we exchanged info. We still never talked until we saw each other again. He and I moved quickly. It was as if we immediately jumped into a situation. I had this thing of always wanting to prove to men that I was worthy.

Therefore, I quickly went into action with him. I started taking on the role of the woman in his life. He never asked me to; I just jumped right into action. Washing his clothes, giving him money, cleaning up his room. I needed him to know that I would do anything for him. I needed to set myself apart from any other women he knew. I also learned this from my mother. She cared for my father in a way none of the other women did, which is why he married her. (I believed this about my short-lived childhood with my parents).

You have already lost when you compete with anyone other than yourself.

It should only ever be you vs. you. I was a college student then, but I was always about getting my money. I would work two or three jobs at one time. I do not know if I was automatically assumed to be a person with money, but he did not hesitate to ask. I also did not hesitate to give it or even offer it.

I also learned this from my mother. She was the breadwinner in our home. While she worked, my dad would sit and gamble all of our money away for hours at a slot machine in a store. This person gambled a lot, too—sometimes all night.

The first time I gave him money, I drove from Orangeburg, SC, to Columbia, SC. That night, I also found a birthday card from a woman who was in love with him. I was doing all this to "prove" myself, and he had other women in his life. Here is where I messed up. I already knew he had other women from my gut feeling. My intuition was present, but I ignored it. *Listen to yourself; you know when you know*

I confronted him about the card. Many dramatics played into that conversation, but not enough for me to walk away. He knew I was willing to do anything for him, which is rare. (So I thought). I also wanted to be a super independent woman. I always wanted anyone I dealt with to know that I could handle it no matter what. It needed to be clear and understood that I always had it, even if I did not. Put the heavy stuff on me. I was building myself this way so that no man could ever say I was using them or that I wanted anything from them but them.

Moment of Transparency—This was just a young-minded way of thinking. It was almost as if I was trying to prove to a man that

I was a man. It was also slight manipulation on my part, as it displayed wanting to be in control. If I am the one with the funds, then I will use that to have more access. On what planet is this?

Wisdom knows that being a damsel in distress and an actor is better (lol). I'm just kidding. However, there is nothing wrong with a woman who exists in her softness. She can be strong and gentle all at once. I assumed that taking care of the men I loved with things displayed that I was an asset.

A Brewing Disaster

Even with me initially being the provider in our relationship, all he did was cheat and lie. The only reason we ended up in a relationship is because he lied. I already knew about the other woman, but he lied again. My investigation began because he once insinuated, after we had just finished being intimate, that he heard I had an STD.

I could have pinpointed his manipulation tactic if I had been a little more logical and less emotional at that moment. It was an attempt to break me down. Abuse never starts with your physical. Your mind comes first.

We had just finished having unprotected sex, and then you accused me of having an STD. How strange! When I asked him, "How did that make sense?" He began to reference that I had a good vagina, so it was worth the risk.

This is where it gets stupid. When he told me that part, it made me feel good. He affirmed me. He told me that he liked something I had enough to risk his health. For me, this was all ego-based. When we exist in our egos, we cannot see anything—not others or ourselves. Therefore, needing and wanting to be affirmed by him was my high priority. I also allowed him to place the value of who I was on my vagina.

Ladies, please do not ever let a man devalue you in this way. Your worth is not based on what a man thinks of you. You determine your worth. Not a man or anyone, for that matter.

He never cared or wanted the truth; he tried to break me. If I felt less than, I was less than. Shame is a common tactic of mental abuse. He knew damn well I did not have an STD. I still wanted to prove him wrong, and I did.

I was tested regularly, so I knew my status, but it became a game of always having to prove myself. I always showed him why I was the better option or valuable enough to be in his life. Once I proved him wrong, I felt more beneficial to him.

My ego again began to be fed. I would do anything to prove I was the better woman. Although this was happening, and I was this way, I could not see that about myself then. I also did not know that I was yearning for this male, fatherly love from a man who was, at the time, incapable of being a good father to his seed.

After I proved myself, we started spending more and more time together—every day. I wanted to be his girlfriend badly, but he never asked or made it official. I began to do everything he wanted me to do, no matter what he asked of me. I even volunteered myself to do more.

Add bailing him out of jail to the list of overall things. The very first time, the bail was $682.00. I had to figure out how to get that quickly. I was a college student working, and that was not a little bit of money at that time. I guess I did not move fast enough because it had been paid when I called to pay.

That evening, I went out and saw his friends. We talked and laughed for a second, but I told one of them I went to make a payment, but the bail was already paid. His friend reassured me that his friend group took care of it. This was a lie.

Quick Note: Ladies, his friends are not your friends. Keep the expectations from his friends low; no matter how "cool" you are with them. This rule has some exceptions, but they are infrequent. Expect that his friends are just that—**his friends.**

I ended up paying all the additional fees and other warrants that were out there. Between all the fees and handling different things, I spent just as much, if not more, than the initial bail amount.

I picked him up late one night after he had just gotten out of jail. It was strange because he randomly called me from a cell phone number I did not recognize. He told me to come and pick him up from the bus stop downtown. Yes, he told me, because he did not ask. Foolishly, like always with him, I got up out of my bed and went. I took him home; he got out of my car and said he would talk to me tomorrow.

My heart slightly dropped. I knew he would want to spend his first night out of jail with me. It had been weeks at this point. However, he did not. I later found out that he spent it with her.

When I speak in her terms, it is usually just one woman. Sometimes, "the her" is another woman (there were many). She also paid his initial bond, so when he got out of jail, he gifted her a Dooney and Burke bag—at the time, that was an "it girl" bag. He also gave her money. I had been giving him money and paying for almost everything for over six months, and he chose to do things for another woman. This would be his first time choosing another woman before me, but certainly not his last.

The First Other Woman

As I previously stated, he cheated with many women, many different times, in our relationship. I guess I never realized how insecure this made me. Over a period, I adjusted my life to being a sideline girlfriend. I was his girlfriend, but I knew he dealt with other women. I also knew he never intended to be honest with me about who he was. He did convey to me before we made it "official" that he did not want to be in a relationship. I should have believed him. However, it is hard to do that when someone says one thing sometimes but does another thing all the time.

We must understand that we should hold value and take up space in any relationship. The love we give should be reciprocated. There was never a moment that I felt like my love was ever valued. Not once in our five years together.

My initial introduction to the other woman was through investigation. I went looking and found exactly what I was looking for. The fact that I became very good at investigating things was unhealthy and took a toll on my mind. It began to consume me. I always wanted to know what he had going on outside of me. This is even more peculiar because when I started investigating, he was not my man, nor were we in a relationship.

When you give your power away to your partner or anyone, you lose who you are. You give your power away by putting yourself through unnecessary stress and trauma. By investigating what he was doing, it brought no resolve. It only added to an already chaotic situation. I was stressing myself out when I was not going to leave.

Once I found out about the other woman, I began searching for precisely who she was. The lie I told myself then was that I had no concrete evidence that he was dealing with her. The truth is I did have evidence. I just wanted more. Why do we do that? If it walks like a duck and quacks like a duck, it damn sure ain't a rabbit. I remember vividly asking him, "Are you talking to other women"?

He always made it a point to let me know he did not have the time to deal with anyone else. I do not know how he managed to deal with both of us, but he did. I finally got the courage to be more specific and say her name to him. He denied her to me. However, now that he knew that I knew, his behavior changed. It seemed like he got a little nicer, a bit softer. He was playing a game, and I was falling for it.

A Night To Remember

She and I were both at a party on a Saturday night; that is what we did every Saturday, we partied. My brother Martin and I went to a club that night called Dreams. It was March 27th, 2010. I remember it because it was my birthday month, also the month we made it official. (Only after I confronted him about the other woman).

He and his friends were throwing a party there that night, so I was going. We had been spending more nights together and most of our time. We would talk on the phone until he fell asleep. I was naturally always up.

I am a night owl; I assume it was her time when I hung up with him. I will never know.

What I did that night reflected how insecure I was. It showed me in a crazy, out-of-pocket way—**all my own decisions.** There were things I had no business doing that night, and approaching this woman was one of them.

I knew that just as I knew who she was, she knew who I was. We were dealing with the same man, and we knew that. Neither of us was his girlfriend yet. As soon as she and her friend walked in, my mind was made up to talk to her. My younger self had no chill. I would fight any time or place. Of course, our initial interaction was laced with drunken sarcasm, but she gave me enough info to head to his apartment. I was not going to talk. I was going to fight him.

Although my brother was with me, I did not tell him I was leaving. This is how furious I was. He never showed up to the party, and that is because he knew both of us were there. I kept calling his phone, but he never answered. I called and texted him so much that my phone started moving slowly.

You should never allow this moment for yourself. When someone shows you how they value you, WALK AWAY if it does not meet your personal value system. Walking away does not require more than that. An explanation is a courtesy when you have been devalued. I was also not his girlfriend; I did not own him even if I had been. He did not belong to me. I was so possessive, but we do not own people. We get to experience them, but they are not our property.

The car ride to his apartment seemed so long. He still never answered my calls or responded to any of my texts. The rage that was inside of me kept growing. Each time he did not answer my call or text, it grew.

My brother started calling and texting me to see where I was. I told him I had to take care of something. He could hear the rage and asked me, "You good?" Martin is not my biological brother, but we are bonded by love. That is my brother. We have been close since we were 15. He knows when something is wrong with me. I kept saying, "I'm good." He kept asking if I was sure. He let me know he had a ride home, but not to forget that his gun was underneath the seat.

Here comes another moment of me losing myself. Once I got to his apartment, I grabbed my brother's gun. With the gun in my hand, I walked to his door and started banging. Here I am, standing at a man who is not my man's door, acting insane with a gun in my hand. I was talking a lot of shit to him through the door, calling him a bitch and a pussy numerous times. I was acting like a savage. I wanted blood. I started kicking the door and banging on it with the gun.

DO NOT EVER LET SOMEONE CONTROL YOU. When someone else angers you, they are in control. I am also thankful to all my angels across different times and spaces because I would have shot him had he opened that door. I can barely tap into the moment because so much rage and infuriation were present. This was all wrapped in hurt feelings.

Back then, when you hurt me, I would hurt myself more by hurting you than by letting you hurt me again. I would become heartless and cold. This was a scary moment for me, but there I was. My whole life up until that point had been filled with countless heartbreak. I wanted him to feel what I felt. All of this was unfortunate for a young woman like me. I was leaning into the man who was a replica of my father, unknowingly repeating a cycle.

He never came to the door, so I returned to my car to sit and wait. I was never leaving. As I sat waiting, the other woman pulled up. She calmly got out of the car, and I got her attention. I got out of my car, and we both began to shake our heads. She asked if I had talked to him, and I told her, "No." I returned the question; she had not spoken to him either.

We both let our guards down briefly and began talking woman to woman. She shared more than I did, but the things I did share were much more serious. I asked if he told her he loved her, and she said, "No, we don't say I love you."

At this point, I started feeling like the scenario's winner. I was so young and naive that I thought that since he told me he loved me and not her, I had this hierarchy in some way. Not loving her meant his "I love you" was real. Since he does not love her, some things she says are false. Right?

His roommate at that time walked up with a girl, and we ran down on him. The girl he was with was about to go off on him until she realized what was happening. He laughed and said, "Ya'll crazy," but he let us in.

She walked in first and called his name. He had been asleep. He woke up but never said anything. She started grabbing things she bought for him, and she walked out. I just sat there staring at him, not saying anything. Then, like an unsuspecting young woman, my rage turned to sadness. I was almost in love with him then, so I was sad. I had done so much for him, handling anything he asked. I made it a point to be anything he wanted me to be, to have him. So, all of this hurt me. Looking back, I can see where I contributed to my heartbreak. I was expecting this loyalty and unwavering love from someone when I did not even love myself. How could I have loved myself? I was allowing this person to do whatever they wanted to me. At the beginning of our situation, he was not doing anything for me, but I was doing everything for him. I was also the one who talked to the other woman and continued giving without any return.

I kept waiting for him to say something. He did not. She doubled back to grab a few more things she had bought. It became apparent we were both looking for answers. As we walked out, he grabbed my arm and whispered, "You stay." I just looked at him, almost in tears, and said," For what"? He looked sad, and I wanted to stay, but he would have to fight for me this time. I needed him to fight for my love; hell, give me anything more than he had been doing.

***A PLACE TO LEARN*—You should never have to fight for someone's love, and no one should have to fight for yours. Love is the highest and most**

absolute vibration. It should be calm, endearing, easy, soft and light.

I did leave because I did not want to be the girl who is played and stays, but in the end, that is exactly the girl I became. My entire ride home was spent deciding to let go of him, and the night was sleepless. When the new day arrived, I decided my questions needed an answer. I no longer cared about just popping up. I honestly felt I had every right.

Easter was approaching the following weekend, so I purchased an Easter basket for his child and went to his apartment to take it to him. Once I got there, the anger had settled, but the sadness was in full force. I was so sad about losing the man I was falling in love with. I do not think he ever really thought I would leave, so he played a role. We talked for hours, and he apologized. He even carved our initials into a tree. (To know me is to know that I love trees, and this move made me forgive him.) He kept reassuring me that "I was his"! After everything that had happened, I felt conflicted about agreeing to be his girlfriend. He told me he was done with her and wanted to start anew.

On that day, we created a form of communication called "the truth tree." Anytime we called it, the moment had to be raw honesty with no consequence. (I never really used the truth tree because he may have harshly punished me if I had.) This was really for him, but it seemed like it would work. We had adopted a system that would help us be good to each other. In my head, I fixed us.

However, I had not even scratched the surface of how much turmoil would consume my life after we became "official." There is a saying: "Be careful what you ask for; you just might get it."

A Downward Spiral

Once we officially started a relationship, things took an interesting turn. I soon found myself in an ugly love triangle that never seemed to end. The other woman was not backing down, but why should she? We had both been repeatedly lied to and manipulated. There were so many lies that they all began to run together. Not only was I being lied to and mentally and emotionally abused, I began to be physically abused as well. The physical abuse began after a long series of me catching him with this other woman repeatedly.

He had already started subtly grabbing me tightly by my arm or pushing his body into mine aggressively. He would try to get me to stand down. He exuded excessive force almost more often than not to try to get me to stop talking once I found things out.

I remember once dreaming that the other woman was at his house. Again, as I stated earlier, I have always had spiritual gifts. My spirit was leading me. I went to his house to find that she was, in fact, there. He kept me from fighting her that day, but the next time I saw her, we fought.*-**Fighting over a man is not it***. My fight should have only been with him; she owed me nothing. He should have gotten all the smoke, not her, not ever. The night I fought her, she was with her friend, so I fought them both. I was also pepper sprayed by security. I felt like I was going blind. Being pepper sprayed is an excruciating, unfathomable pain.

He knew we were fighting because the brawl began inside the club right in front of him. He never left the party to check on me or see if I was okay, and he never called me that night. My cousin's husband happened to be there and made sure I made it to my destination safely.

A few years before this relationship, I was in a relationship with someone else, and that night, he took care of me. Imagine falling into the arms of someone else who is no good to you. This person abused me mentally and emotionally as well. Trauma had me running back to men, even though they had hurt me. I had nowhere else to turn, but he ensured I was okay. He also held me as I cried and made sure I made it home. I kept falling into these toxic holes. It was becoming harder to dig myself out. That night, I just wanted to feel loved, and he gave that to me. I was such a sad soul.

The one question he asked me that night that stuck with me was, "How can you be with somebody who doesn't protect you"? I had no answer for him because I did not have an answer for myself. I had never been with someone who protected me. I did not know what that looked like. I stayed up all night crying and thinking. I thought about every detail of that evening. I thought about how sorry he was and how every single time I saw this other woman, I was going to whoop her ass. What initially started as anger towards him ended up being anger towards her.

Most women who are dealing with a man who has multiple women have this problem. They take it out on the other woman, and the man gets to live freely and exist in toxicity. We always have misguided anger towards the woman solely because she, too, has what we have and want for ourselves. We must learn to be honest with who and what we are in every moment.

The Who: Who am I to this person? Who is this person to me? Who is this person in my world? I knew who I thought he was, but I needed to figure out who I was to him. Who he told me I was and who I actually was were different.

The What: What am I to this person? Identify yourself. What is this person to me? What purpose do they serve here? What is this person here to teach me? What am I learning from this person? Answering these questions truthfully can save time.

I gave in and called him the following day, but he did not answer. I sent him this long message about being done and that I no longer wanted to be a part of his games. I felt so humiliated.

He responded that afternoon, and while I wanted to ignore him the way he had ignored me, I just could not. I needed answers. Now, from my perspective on cheating, I really should have allowed him to do so in peace. I was not going to leave him, so why create more chaos? I never intended to leave him, no matter what he did to me. Even today, I cannot say that infidelity is the ultimate deal breaker for me. I think we are all human, and sometimes we make mistakes. If you are a habitual, disrespectful liar, I will say no. We are all different when it comes to cheating. You must make the best decision based on **your** personal deal-breakers. At this particular time in my life, I acted as if I had deal-breakers, but I did not.

Once he responded, it was just an ongoing argument. He kept trying to explain himself and to get me to see things from his viewpoint. He kept lying about her to me. I remember the tears turning into extreme anger. I kept asking him, "How could you leave me alone while I'm fighting two people?" His constant response was, "I did not know." He was still lying. Not only did he know, he deliberately continued to party and ignore me. The whole argument started right in front of him. I hung up on him many times during that conversation, and he also hung up on me.

Again, existing in toxic chaos to say, "He's mine." Sometimes, we would stop calling and texting, get back on the phone, and yell. The both of us just hollering on the phone. Hours passed of this same trend. I finally sat down and logged in from my computer to Facebook. The year was 2010, so we still logged onto Facebook from computers. I had a message from the other woman:

<u>**MAY 9TH, 2010 @ 4:47 PM**</u>

I JUST WANT YOU TO KNOW… YOU FUCKING FIGHTING ME OVER A NIGGA… WHO APARTMENT I BE OVER EVERY NIGHT… THAT WAS CATERING TO ME LAST NIGHT…MAKING SURE I WAS GOOD AFTER THE WHOLE SITUATION… DAMN, MOVE ON TO THE NEXT ONE… BC REGARDLESS _____ IS STILL GOING TO DEAL WITH ME….

I must have read this message a thousand times. I kept replaying how he left me with a pepper-sprayed face. I remember screaming aloud, ***"THAT STUPID MOTHERFUCKER"***. I was enraged.

I wanted to fight both of them at this point. Again, hurt feelings. It happened repeatedly. He never mentioned her being at his house or that she was with him the night we fought, but why would he? He was in a relationship with two women at this point. I called him, and when he answered, I just started yelling. I was also crying, so I am sure it came out as gibberish. I specifically kept saying, "I'm done. You played the fuck out of me. She was over there?" "You let that bitch come over there, and you left me alone?"

I am not proud of the person I would become when provoked. There was so much hurt and anger inside of me. I grabbed my keys and headed to his place. I was going to fight him. He kept calling me, but I never answered. He started texting me, telling me to answer.

I finally answered." What the fuck do you want; I'm coming to you right now." However, he was not there. He had moved. He never told me he was moving. We were in a relationship, and he never once told me anything. I never even had the address; he just guided me there.

Once I get there, I hop out and immediately start hitting him in the face. I should have never put my hands on him. No matter how mad I was. Domestic disputes should never happen on either party's behalf.

He again gaslighted me and lied about not telling me he moved. I was told she was only around to finance his move. She volunteered to help pay for everything, so he used her help.

This should have been a huge red flag for me. Why would I ever want to be with a man who used another woman, or anyone for that matter? Why would I not think he would do this to me? I ignored every red flag.

1) Allowing two women he dealt with to fight
2) Lying to me every chance he could
3) Not even having enough courtesy to tell me he moved
4) Leaving me unprotected both emotionally and physically.
5) Telling me he was using another woman for monetary gain.

Each red flag was ignored because I wanted the man. I needed to beat her to have him. Foolishly, I stayed with him that night after all of that. After all of the emotional abuse we both endured that entire day, I made my choice to stay. I believed every single "I am sorry" I heard all day. I immediately went into what I learned from my father. This was my response to men who hurt me. First, I would feel bad. Next, I would let them make me feel bad, and then, I would run back to them even though they had just hurt me.

Apologies should come with changed behavior. This apology did not. I knew in my heart he would continue to deal with her, but this had also become a game for me. I lost trust in him, but I needed to play this game and win.

I think a lot of wasted energy and time comes from playing games. I thought I was playing a game to win; I was playing myself. The games continued because I responded to the other woman's message once I got home. I still needed to save face and tell her I was not moved or worried.

May 10th, 2010 @ 8:43 PM

I FOUGHT YOU OVER RESPECT>>>> I DO NOT CARE ABOUT YOU OR _____. WHATEVER U CHOOSE TO DO IS FINE WITH ME SWEETIE... UNDERSTAND THAT YOU WERE ONLY WITH HIM BECAUSE I ALLOWED YOU TO BE... DON'T TELL ME TO MOVE ON TO SHIT, CAUSE I DO WHAT THE FUCK I WANT TO. I, BONITA RENEA JONES AM GIVING HIM TO YOU. IF THIS IS THE MAN THAT YOU WANT TO BE WITH _____ OK. YOU AS A WOMAN SHOULD WANT BETTER. BUT I SEE THAT UR THE TYPE WHO LIKES THIS GUY DRAMA THING. THE TYPE TO GET PREGNANT BY A MAN TO KEEP HIM. THAT'S NOT CUTE SWEETHEART. VALUE YOURSELF MORE. BY NO MEANS DO I GIVE A FUCK WHAT YALL DO WHEN YALL DO IT. I AM A STRONG WOMAN... UR A WALKING CONTRADICTION. U PUT UP STATS ABOUT LETTING GO AND HOW INSECURE WOMEN STAY AND CONFIDENT WOMEN LEAVE AND YET UR IN THE SAME PLACE U ALWAYS HAVE BEEN. YOU SEE THE DIFFERENCE IN YOU AND ME IS, WHEN I SAY, I'M GONNA DO SOMETHING I DO IT PERIOD. U WRITING ME WAS PRETTY POINTLESS SEEING AS I COULD GIVE TWO FLYING SHITS ABOUT WHAT YOU AND _____ DO. BELIEVE

ME WHEN I TELL U, HANDING OVER THIS HEADACHE IS FINE. THE SAME WAY U "THINK" HE'S ALL ABOUT YOU, HE IS NOT... HE IS ALL ABOUT HIS SELF. DO URSELF A FAVOR AND DON'T BE A DUMB GIRL... ALSO DO URSELF A FAVOR AND KEEP MY NAME OUT UR MOUTH. U HAVE NO REASON TO WORRY ABOUT ME. LUCKILY FOR YOU I AM GOING TO BE MATURE ABOUT THIS AND CALL MY GOONS OFF YOUR ASS, CAUSE THIS SITUATION WAS GONNA GET WORSE BEFORE IT GOT BETTER. ALSO UNDERSTAND THAT THIS BURDEN YOU WANT SO MUCH, IS GONNA DO THE SAME TO YOU. DON'T BE A BLONDE, AND AFTER I WRITE THIS I COULD CARE LESS WHAT YALL TALK ABOUT OR DO... I DO NOT CARE LET ME SAY THIS AGAIN, I DO NOT CARE.

I WISH YALL BLISS AND ALL THAT GOOD SHIT... AND ALSO DO NOT WRITE ME BACK, CAUSE AS OF NOW UR A NON EXISTENCE TO ME, AND IM ENDING THIS WITH A PERIOD... (WHICH MAKES. THIS A STATEMENT, NOT A QUESTION) WHICH MEANS DON'T REPLY.

Well, that was long-winded, LOL. She should have said, "Girl, I ain't reading all that". Looking back at this message now, I was so bothered. I kept trying to convince myself I did not care, but I cared **A LOT**. I was too embarrassed to say anything other than that. She could not have one up on me.

I could also recognize that I wanted more in the space I was in—I wanted to be more. I kept trying to advise her when I needed to take my advice. We often cannot see ourselves while we are right in the thick of it. We can see and name everyone else's flaws but not our own.

I was staring right at my reflection. This back and forth continued for months to come. Our arguments and subliminal context to each other moved from Facebook to Twitter. The guy and I ended up moving in together, and the cheating continued. It may have even gotten worse. I always knew about the other women because I would look through his phone. Sometimes, I lied and said someone told me something, but no one ever did. I knew because I went looking.

As a reminder: When you look for things, you find them. I had no intention of leaving. I was constantly torturing myself by going through his phone, which was an unhealthy practice. I did not recognize my worth or who I was, so I allowed the cheating and disrespect to continue. I always spoke up about my issues with the relationship, but I never put action behind my words. I was searching for love and companionship with this person, but I could not give that love to myself. Never once did I choose myself while with him. Eventually, I fought back the only way I knew how.

Cheating Back

I will preface this by saying I never wanted to cheat. I was doing something to make myself feel less stupid then. I was not strong enough to leave, but I could at least cheat to make myself feel better about being publicly embarrassed repeatedly.

It only made me feel better for a moment, and then I realized this was a temporary fix. I did not even cheat correctly. I made the mistake of cheating with someone that I loved dearly; in turn, I was only making my life more chaotic. I kept bringing people into my world of destruction.

The person I was with never cared enough to notice (or at least he never said anything if he did) except when he said something with two other friends. They sat me down as if I was a kid in the principal's office because of a DM from a friend. This friend and I had nothing going on. This whole encounter was wild because I started to feel like I had done something wrong by responding to the message. He said he had them there, so he would not get physical with me. The irony is that he cheated on me every single day, and he had a round table for a DM. I can truly see how these manipulation tactics often made me more forgiving of him after he cheated. He would mess up, I would find out, and give him the easiest of consequences (me leaving for the weekend sometimes). I am unsure how that is a consequence for a habitual cheater, but it made sense then.

He would ask for my forgiveness, often with a gift attached. No different from my father giving me snacks to keep me quiet about his abuse of my mother. I would forgive him, and then we would exist in time and space like nothing happened—a constant ongoing cycle of bullshit. Our relationship was rooted in lies. There were no truths there. The physical abuse began very early, as early as he moved into the new apartment.

I particularly remember one day he had gotten angry with me for saying, "Well, I'm about to start fucking too, since all you do is fuck bitches". This was in response to me finding out about another other woman.

I tried leaving, but he would not let me. I did everything to escape him; however, he was so strong. I managed to get outside, and he followed me. I even tried to run, but he caught me and slammed me up against the brick wall. He then grabbed my neck and lifted me off the ground. My back was scrubbing the brick.

He did it so hard it tore a hole in my shirt, and my back had what looked like a burn on it, down to the white meat. I remember yelling, "My back, I can't breathe; you're hurting me." He never flinched. He just held me there for a second with this scary look. I said his name, and he snapped back into himself. He kept saying he did not mean to do it; he even went as far as helping me aid the burn. I am crying at this point, but I take his assistance. Again, we acted as if nothing happened.

I began lying to my family about scars and bruises that would pop up on my body. I even lied to them about him throwing my dog off the porch. He bought me a dog, and then, in an attempt to hurt me, he threw her off the porch. That burn on my back was the first visible scar on me. He got good at physically abusing me to where marks would not be seen. I never connected this to abuse because I would fight him back. I would even hit him in anger, no matter where we were. My abuse to him would only come after I would find out about other women. It is not an excuse, but that is why I also never felt like I was this helpless woman being abused. My mother did not fight my father back, so I felt like she was weak. I could never be like her. (This was my internal dialogue.) I thought that abuse translated as helplessness. I was wrong.

While living together, it got worse. He would hold me down at knifepoint, choke me, and he would put me underneath the cover (while I was in a panic) like he was suffocating me. This was his go-to because he knew I hated this the most. How vile and sick do you have to be to try to torture someone with suffocation?

His friends and my cousin lived with us. I often wondered why his friends never jumped in more to save me while all this was happening. Now, I understand why. Victims must be ready to leave; otherwise, it can go badly. Someone can get hurt for trying to step in. It was also better not to involve others, as I had no intention of leaving. It was not their responsibility to advocate for me. I needed to do that for myself.

It happened so often that it was just another fight between us—that is all we did most of the time. My cousin De'Anna would usually knock on the door to stop the fighting, and she saved me many times.

The moments of shame continued to pile up. One unforgettable night, my cousin hung out with a young woman who worked with us. I was the assistant manager, so I also got a job for my cousin. The girl ended up at my house. I did not want her there but did not make a fuss about it. I thought she was cool.

We all were drinking that night, as we usually did. I was often always the one to tap out first. This night, in particular, he kept giving me shots on top of shots. I passed out drunk. I woke up afterward, kind of in a daze, still with all of my clothes on. I got up and looked around; he was not in the bed.

By this time, it was a little after 2 a.m. He should have been in bed. I opened the door to leave the room; it was dark throughout the house. The hallway was long, yet you could hear someone open the door. However, I was not the only person who lived there, and he knew I had passed out drunk.

As I walk towards the living room, I hear faint moans. I become curious about who is having sex in my house, in my living room. My steps got lighter and lighter as I walked towards the couch. We had a sectional, so you could not see around it. I looked over the couch and saw him behind her. I did not know what he was doing, but I immediately assumed he was having sex with her.

I immediately jumped over the couch and lunged at her. He looked up as if he had seen a ghost but grabbed me so fast that he caught me before I connected to her. Once he grabbed me, I began to hit him repeatedly. I was fighting him. Instead of hitting me back, he kept dodging my hits. He kept telling me to "chill" and "calm down," but I could not. **How could he do this in the home we shared?**

The next few moments were a blur. He kept holding me back until we were in the kitchen. I am still yelling and fighting him. He put his arm around my neck and began choking me until it was darkness.

I wake up to firm yet gentle slaps across my face. I gasp for air, and I am lying on the kitchen floor in his arms. He is looking at me very scared and gentle. It was different from his normal glance. He is talking to me, but I cannot hear him because I have blocked out his voice.

I look at him and say, "You are just like my daddy." My entire childhood trauma began to haunt me. At this very moment, he looked exactly like my dad to me. So many thoughts began to run through my head. The loudest question was," **How could you pick somebody like your dad?**" I had few words to say, but here we were again. In some way, he made me feel like I did not see what I knew I saw with my own two eyes. It was such a weird moment because I started to believe that maybe I was making it all up in my mind. He manipulated me into thinking that I had lost my mind.

That night, I did many wrong things—lunging at the girl and fighting him. I had no idea of my self-worth then. It should have been a "no-brainer" moment to pack my bags and leave. I could have felt anger and rage, but none of the dramatics attached to it were necessary, mainly since I stayed.

Something inside of me never wanted to give up on him. I wanted to be the one he changed for and gave everything to. I knew he was still lying to me, but I stayed. My trauma now was all wrapped up into one. Every single part of my childhood was starting to come up in this relationship, including nonconsensual sex.

Writing out these lurid details is extremely hard for me, but when you free yourself, you do it in full, raw form. I do not think I looked at it in its true form at that time. The more I have grown, the more I realize I did not consent. We like to hide behind walls as a community and protect the people we love.

Sometimes, I would wake up from drunken, black-out nights to dry semen on my body. My alcohol tolerance was extremely low. When I would drink, if I did not stop myself, I could get drunk very quickly and easily. Waking up to dried semen on my body happened often. Sometimes it would be on the inside of my legs, but most times, it would be on my butt. I began to notice, so I asked about it. I would always be told "No," sometimes even "Hell no". I was never mad or upset when I asked him. I thought he would naturally tell me.

One day, when he thought I was taking shots, getting drunk. I was not. I wanted to know what was going on, so I pretended to be intoxicated and went to our room. I was lying down, waiting for him. It took about an hour or so for him to come in, and I was unprepared for what happened next.

I could not see what he was doing. I had to lay there and pretend to be drunk. My eyes were closed, but he began to undress me. Once undressed, he started rubbing his penis across my lips softly. He then began to try to force his penis into my mouth.

"What the fuck is he doing"? That was my first thought. "Why won't he just wake me up?" "Is he really going to force his penis into my mouth"? I did not want him to, so I pretended to roll over to stop him. He came and got in the bed naked.

I felt his body next to mine, and then he flipped me on my back and began to penetrate me. As I lay there pretending to be drunk, I felt tears starting to form in my eyes, but I could not flinch.

Usually, when we had sex, we did so from the back. He usually never liked missionary. Well, at least not with me. Therefore, his having sex with me while I was passed out drunk, lying lifeless in a missionary position, was weird to me. He was forcing my legs open to enjoy himself.

Usually, he ejaculated inside of me. Not this time, he pulled out and finished on me. I just lay there, still in slight shock and disbelief. He got a washcloth, wiped me off very quickly, turned off the light, and got in the bed.

I called it sex to justify it in my mind. "Technically, he is my boyfriend, so he has the right." I just kept thinking, "We have sex anyway". This, however, was sexual penetration carried out against a person without consent. I kept my eyes closed until I eventually fell asleep. I woke up the following day, went to the restroom, and as all the other times, there was dried semen on me. I asked him, "Hey, did you have sex with me last night?" Again, I was told, "No." I doubled back and tried to make it more humorous. So I say jokingly; did we have sex then because it's a nut on my leg"? It was still denied. I close the door, shower, and pretend nothing ever happened. This became a full circle moment when someone I love dearly and would die for told me he tried to do the same to her. I knew she was not lying. All the details sounded very familiar. He denied it when I confronted him, and I stayed with him.

The following two years of my life continued in utter ruckus. I was verbally, mentally, emotionally, and physically abused most times on the daily. We argued and fought A LOT. The next series of events took place over two years.

1) I consoled him after finding out his best friend at the time had been dealing with his first "other woman." : I talked him through his heartbreak, which broke him down. I felt like I was real for allowing him the space to grieve losing a friend. He also loved her. I could not tell what hurt him most, knowing he was done with her for good or losing his friend. I safeguarded my feelings by believing the latter.
2) He verbally and physically abused me in front of our peers. : He pushed me off a couch in front of a young woman I respected. He never spared my feelings in front of people.
3) Being arrested and taken to jail for fighting the other woman, as well as being federally indicted: I fought the other woman a second time, and she pressed charges. Later in life, once she and I both grew, she apologized, and I did the same. We both understood our issue was never with each other. I was glad to have a moment of womanhood with her. I want her to know that I wish her immense love and light, and I am thankful that she and I found love and ourselves. Neither of us deserved that: I was federally indicted and told I could spend up to two years in prison. Turning myself in and being fingerprinted felt like one of my life's most significant failures. I had allowed this man to manipulate me into something wrong. Our home was raided, and I used the iPad notes section as a journal. That is one of the pieces of evidence that saved me. I talked about hating to do it and only doing it because I loved him. My lawyer used that to defend me.
4) Finding out about another woman: He loved her, too. He talked to her every day while I went to work and he sat home unemployed.
5) Him trying to prostitute me to a bails bondsman to get him out of jail. : He was in jail in Alabama. He gave me the information for a bail bondsman. I drove there and met with the

man. I was about $1000 short. The bondsman was a middle-aged white man. He explained that he could get him out, but when people were short, they did other things instead. I immediately understood what other things meant. I was not prepared to do that. When he called me and asked me the status of getting out, I explained to him that it seemed like the man wanted to have sex with me. He told me to do what I had to do. He was only concerned about getting out of jail. I started crying. I went back to the bail bondsman with red eyes. As I walked in, he asked me, "Are you ok"? I started crying and told him, "I was not prepared for any of this, but I have to get my boyfriend out of jail." He explained that he did not want to take advantage of the situation that way. He said most people that came to him knew exactly why they were coming to him. He did rub on my back and touched my leg a lot while he was talking to me. I was inconsolable. I am not sure why that man helped me that day. I do not know if it was his guilt or just my angel watching out for me.
6) Constantly being told, "I love you to death," and understanding precisely what that meant. : He said it when he was mad and when he was not. He played with it and said it so much that it became his mantra.

I cannot entirely blame him for the things I endured. It was also my fault for staying and continuing the cycle. He showed me exactly who he was from day one. I chose to look over all of that and stay.

I often asked him, "Why do you keep doing this to me?" Why do you keep hurting me?" The problem is that I never asked myself those questions. I never stopped to think of the role I played in our relationship. The physical abuse stopped once my uncle LeVar intervened. He protected me for what felt like the first time in my life. I will forever be grateful to him for loving me that way.

The relationship needed to end, but I could not gather the strength for some strange reason. I also could not see how my life had become another cycle. I was becoming my mother. I started to ask myself, "How can you let your mother's death be in vain?" "Why didn't you learn from your mama?" **"Would she be proud of you?"** This question plagued me the most.

Detailing these events in my life is not about atonement. It is about displaying how trauma can wrap you in. It also gives details about how the chaos started. We established a relationship in turmoil. The relationship had nowhere to grow. Trust was never present. As much as I wanted love to be present, it never was.

I could sit here and bash him for everything done to me over five years, but you learn to take accountability with growth. You hold yourself responsible for what happens to you.

I am not a victim. I allowed this to happen because I never loved myself enough to choose me. Havoc and pain were familiar to me. "This is just how it goes. "You fight for love." "No relationship is perfect."

These were my self-soothers. We were also young. This is also important to note.

You would think almost going to prison is when I would wake up. I did not realize its seriousness. I was going to be his ride or die, no matter what. A good friend, more like a brother, told me, "Black, you're being dumb, and it still was not clicking. I could never believe that sticking by the man I loved was dumb.

Had I looked at everything that happened before he went to prison with honest lenses, I would have left without a trace, no longer accessible to him. I could not see myself. I felt trapped in the bullshit with nowhere to turn. It was not until another woman's truth was revealed that I finally said, "I'm done."

I had known about her for a while. I did a thorough investigation to figure out exactly who she was. She came about a year after the first other woman. I found out about her by seeing a video of them having sex. I found it in his phone and later connected her to a face, then a name.

I was unsure until I called her friend and line sister, who told me everything about them. I was about to burn all his clothes and shoes until my best friend stopped me.

Learning Point: We should never allow what we already know to get the best of us. I already knew he was dealing with her, and I had a phone bill to prove it, among other things. I should have never addressed this with him if I had no intention of leaving or resolving the issues.

I was getting a little stronger because, this time, I did not take it to the other woman. I took it up with him. My issue was never with the women. A deeper dive into that: My issue was with me. I was the problem—not him, not them, just me.

After his continuous lies, telling me he no longer talked to her, my life changed when the federal indictment came for us both. Many moments went into this period—more untold truths, lies, deception, and drama.

I was given somewhat of a Pre-trial intervention type of program on a federal level. I had no prior record, only a pending charge from the fight between the first other woman and me. I was also not the person they truly wanted.

By The Most High's protection and The Universe, I was paroled for 18 months. After three years, my record was expunged. He went to prison, and for the first six months, I held him down unapologetically, even though he had sex with another woman right before he turned himself in. I found this out by looking through his phone again. I still felt I owed this to him, and I could not be one of those girls who leave a man when he is down. I put all my feelings aside to be there for him.

While he was away, I checked the other woman's tweets to see if she talked to him. One day, "NOT TO MY SURPRISE," she mentioned a letter. She would retweet her friend's tweets about it being a love letter. I immediately knew he had written to her. It was so odd that he had written her a letter when he had not even called me his first week there. It was as if he was mad at me for being on the outside while he was locked up.

A sudden shift happened for me at that moment. I realized this was something I no longer wanted to do. After all these years of everything I dealt with in the relationship, it was this one defining moment that I had a sudden change of heart. A true testament to, when you are done, you are just done. No explanation.

When we spoke about it, my new awakening was tested. I told him I knew about the letter and did not want to have this relationship anymore. I was confident in my stance—I was finally standing up for myself.

I wanted to cry, but the tears never fell. He did not lie to me about the letter because he knew that I already knew the truth. He tried to smooth things over with me. He sent me letters from prison, begging me to stay. He even had some of his peers in the prison write me on his behalf. I also spoke to this other woman. He finally confessed his truth to her, and she and I both had a moment in womanhood. Again, my issues were never with them. He could have gotten me back into a typical interaction with us, BUT NOT THIS TIME. This time, not even our unborn child, which I miscarried in 2013, could keep me there as it used to. I realized that if I stayed here any longer, I would die.

Healing Points

1) *When someone shows You who they are, you must see them for just that.*

This can save so much time and unnecessary pain and strife. Believing who that person is and not who you want or expect them to be is critical. We often think we can change people. People have to want to change themselves. Growth comes from doing the inner work. When they are ready to evolve, they will. This is not up to you.

2) If you have to dig for something, maybe rethink if this is your safe space.

This may not be a place where you can thrive without question. Time often reveals all tales. Remember that.

3) Do not be afraid to walk away.

Walk away from the things that do not serve you. Be honest with yourself about who you are. You do not have to stay in a place that drowns you. It is counterproductive to your advancement in life.

4) People are not your property.

We are all here on borrowed time. People are here to inspire, love, and live here with us. However, we do not own those we love; we do get to experience them.

5) Addressing another man/woman about someone you are directly involved with shows more about who you are.

Address the person you are dealing with and create a safe space for change. Then, decide to either stay or go. Also, understand the importance of this choice.

6) Do not ever let someone tell you who you are.
You have to show people how to love and treat you. People do not get the chance to pick how you should be treated. You demand it. Doing this will show you who you are, as well as those around you.

7) *Break generational cycles.*
We must break those generational curses that were never ours. So often, we carry our parents' generational curses, and they carry their parents' generational curses, and so on. Choosing to say, "This will be my legacy" or "This will be what I create" is so powerful. We no longer bear burdens that were never ours to carry in the first place.

ERA THREE

When a Flower Blooms

Starting Over

Let us back up a bit; right before I decided to be done, some moments shaped my new life. When I came back from seeing him off to prison, I had absolutely nothing: no car, nowhere to live, and no money.

Everything we had together was gone. My life was in complete shambles. I did not know what to do or how to get myself out of this. I was completely lost and had nothing to show for five years. Of all the money, cars, designer purchases, and lavish lifestyle, I had NOTHING. I started to crumble. As stated previously, he never spoke to me the first week he was in prison. That first week, I was a wreck. I cried so much I did not think any tears were left.

I had no car, so I walked to and from work. I worked at a hotel near my old apartment and aunt's house. The morning I returned to work after being gone for two weeks, I began calculating my life and expenses. I realized I did not have anywhere to go.

My Aunt Renea allowed me to move in with her to get myself back on my feet. She also told me I had to pay her $300 monthly to live there. I remember being so mad at her for charging me to stay with her because I had nothing.

Looking back on it now, I needed that lesson. I also looked at my credit score that morning. It was 389. I remember seeing it and my knees slightly buckling while I bent over at the front desk. I was gasping for air. I did not know a credit score could get so low.

I realized that every unpaid loan, opened credit card accounts, and horrible financial decision I had made over the years in the relationship were coming back to haunt me—all of which were choices that I made.

Standing back up, I stared at the computer for about ten minutes. I was sitting there trying to figure out how my life had gotten this far out of control. "How in the hell had I let it get this bad"? I began thinking.

I was always prepared for life (so I thought), but I had no control over it this time. As I walked home from work that day, I decided to fight for myself as best as possible.

Standing Still

As much as I wanted to fight for myself, all I could seem to do at that moment was stand still. I did not have much going on. I only worked and went home. For the first six months, I saved money. I was not making much money, but I made enough to maintain a little bit of a life.

I had never done this before. I had never stood still at any point in my life. Every moment was moving, busy, and doing something at all times. However, I stood still for six months in a cubby I had created.

I did not move. I had to replenish my plant.

Learning Myself

Amidst standing still, I started learning who I was and what I wanted and did not want out of life—this transitional moment prepared me for what was next. It was time for me to face myself. In every possible way, I had to face myself. I had to begin to understand and realize the role I played in my life being in shambles. I understood, "Bonita, you also had something to do with this." Indeed, one of my most challenging and endearing teachers.

Taking Accountability

One of the hardest things for humans to do is hold themselves accountable. It is an arduous moment because you begin to realize how shitty you are. (Well, in my case). I was not the human I proclaimed to be. I was not perfect in my old relationship. I did things as well. I had no intention of growing or changing because I could not recognize my role in my life spiraling down.

I also had to assess my attitude. I was very self-absorbed. You could not tell me that I was not "That Girl." I wanted so badly to be her, but at that time, I was not. Being "That Girl" does not require you to do anything but exist in your light. You do not have to be mean or unkind to be her. It truly is an inside job.

On my accountability journey, I was faced with my unhealed trauma. It was lingering inside of me. I began to ask, "Why Bonita?" "Why did you do this?" "Why aren't you being responsible for how you live? "Why are you allowing this to be your story"?

While doing this part, I was still in love with someone. I never thought in a million years that we would not end up together while I was doing all of this self-work. I was willing to stand the test of time and be the woman who held it down. I still wanted us to work.

This was rooted in time. I had spent all this time with this person; I did not want to start over. I kept telling myself, "This is normal couples shit, and nobody is perfect."

However, once the phone call about the letter happened, I immediately said, "This is no longer for me." Even with everything that had happened until that point, that should have been an ("ah-ha") moment.

The confirmation from that phone call was my moment of revolution, my moment of rebellion. It was time for me to show myself who I was. I had to pick my life back up and become the woman I always thought I was.

The Transformation

Once I let go of what no longer served me, more things about my life began to make sense. The why became much more evident. I started doing the work to ensure that I could not only answer this question but also face it without fear, shame, or doubt.

My Spiritual Journey

I began a spiritual journey of learning myself all over again and starting to love myself. I began to care more about my health—not just my physical health but what was happening inside me.

My mental, emotional, and spiritual health all had to align. I was raised in the church, so I know who God is, but I had to walk my path to come directly back to spirit. I began to understand that God lives within. I started to strip away what I thought my relationship with God should look like and started to have one.

I started talking to The Most High about healing and growing. I always came back to myself on that." What work are you putting in to grow yourself"? "How are you helping yourself heal?" "How are you changing you for the better?" "What steps are you taking to love yourself on the journey?" I kept digging into myself more and more. This was also not a journey of all smiles and sunshine. This journey was hard and long. It required more of me than I have ever given and improved my life.

Meditation

My Aunt/Mother Bonita introduced me to meditation for the first time. She introduced it to me in 2013. The first time I did meditation, I fell asleep. I did not understand everything about it, so I was uninterested. It was not until 2016 that I made a lifestyle change. I no longer wanted to live the same and needed a new resource. I started to learn. I learned about the effectiveness of Meditation and began using those tools. I began to center myself and learn oneness. Oneness allowed me to be comfortable with being alone. I got so close with THE MOST HIGH that I began doing the things I loved most again.

Once I began to develop my walk with God, I no longer needed to be validated in my faith. I understood my faith was genuine, and so was God. I did not need a building to get closer to God. I had become a direct reflection of everything I wanted to become.

I no longer had to fight for a spot as God's favorite because I became my favorite, and God lives within me. The Most High had been here all along. I had just been running from myself and could not see that.

Service

Realizing your purpose in life is something most people seek to find. I have naturally always been a servant to people. Whether that is sticking my neck out for them, giving my last, or helping them to grow and evolve.

Looking back on my life, there has never been a moment where I was not serving. After getting closer to myself, I became more involved in community work and helping those around me.

My best friend Quiya and I started a nonprofit organization called The M.A.S.C.A.R.A Project. It was geared towards young girls ages 12–18. We wanted them to become socially aware, politically astute, and positive additions to their communities.

I also began to dive deep into activism for my people and community. This season allowed me to get as close to my people as possible and love them. Giving love freely with no expectations grew me a lot. I learned many lessons while working with people who had less than I did. It humbled me unimaginably and was a core realization of our connection. No matter how different our lives are, we are a community.

Trying to Figure It Out

As time passed, I became increasingly engulfed in learning myself. I no longer wanted to give myself subpar love. I wanted to love myself unconditionally without boundaries, to exist in my highest vibration fully. In doing so, I had to love myself first so that the love I yearned for and gave could be mirrored. It was also important to me to love myself healthily. I started affirming myself daily. I would write affirmations on Post-it notes and put them all over my mirror. Manifesting the life I wanted and deserved began to be an everyday mission.

And So, It Began

I began to see myself, love myself, and advocate for myself. This was the hard part, the dirty part. I started with unpacking my childhood trauma. Whew! What a tough thing to do. The trauma of my childhood had taken its toll on me for far too long. I am an adult now. I could no longer allow the trauma caused in my childhood to interfere with this new, healthy, and thriving woman. This could no longer be an excuse for poor decision-making skills.

I was responsible for every decision that I made and did not make. I began fine-tuning myself. I lost everything, but I got it all back. I made my first big girl purchase and got a car, a new place, a new job, and I started to see myself for the first time. I worked my ass off to prove to myself that I could do anything. Up until that point in my life, my heart had been broken repeatedly, but the beauty of all this was that I was not broken. I was more than enough. I was more than loved, and I was love. I exuded it, so I became it. For so long, I hid in the shadows of who I was meant to be. I used to live in fear and constant chaos in my early childhood and adult life. I wanted to free myself, so I did.

I kept working on myself, getting better and better. As time passed, I grew. There is a moment in growth when you have to say goodbye to the old you, and it is heartbreaking but also rejuvenating.

Initially, it is a little hard to grasp, but you must grow to change. You are shedding a layer, taking you on a journey of your highest self. Moreover, when you do, you truly evolve into the best version of yourself.

I wanted to be better, so I became better and forgave myself for all the times I did not see myself. These were two instrumental years in my journey, 2014–2016. They were very tough years in lessons.

I learned so much, and I just kept growing. Loving me meant accepting all of my pieces—all of my flaws and complex parts, too. I kept falling back into myself. I gave myself pure love. ***The light may have been dim, but it was still a light.***

Oh yeah, ***I fell in love, too***, and created a beautiful family. I cannot wait to share that story with you all (in the next book, wink) because the story is still being written, and I am a different person now.

Healing Points

1) *Understanding your breaking point.*
We often ignore our breaking points until we feel completely broken into two. However, they are not as sad as we make them. They are the moments when we gain strength and courage to evolve, grow, and begin to see who we are.

2) It's ok to stop.
It is ok to stop and reset. Because we exist in the human experience, we tend to be wrapped up in always doing something, always on the move. Sometimes, we must stop and do a little self-work. When you stop moving, also take that time to work on yourself.*

3) Give yourself to the community.
*Giving back is the easiest thing any of us can do. It keeps us thriving as humanity. We are responsible in this world to care for each other as best we can. We do not all do it, but nothing is ever too big or small, and we all must work together. Ujima.

4) Shadow Work
*As someone who once lived in the shadows, I know this is not a part you can run from in healing. You must hold your chin up and chest out when facing your shadows. Honesty about who you are can organically grow you. You can not solve a problem you do not think you have. You must be honest about who you are and want to be.

5) Talking to the source.
*Your relationship with The Higher Being connects you back to yourself. If you develop a solid foundation with the source, you will always be on

the right path because God lives within. Nurture the relationship, protect it, and utilize our resources here on earth. God gave us these things to use.

6) Never Stop Growing.

*Just as the healing journey never ends, neither does growth. Do not ever stop growing and learning. Teach yourself, and equip yourself with as much knowledge as you can. Evolution is necessary, and so is change. Growth has to happen for you to experience them both. When you grow, help the other people around you grow, too.

7) You vs You

In this game of life, it is always you versus you. Comparing your story to someone else's story is counterproductive. Each day, you must work to be a better version of yourself. There is no one created like you. You are a direct reflection of The Most High's love. Remember exactly who you are. What is meant for you will never not be yours. The goal is to be a better version of who you were yesterday. Challenge yourself to get better and better over time. Nobody is going to save you but you.

FROM MY HEART TO YOURS

I hope my story can encourage someone to fight, love, and honor themselves**. I AM NOT PERFECT**. I still make mistakes and am flawed to this day, but I learn. I learn in each moment that is sent to test me. I also learn in each moment that I am not my best self. I now give myself the grace that I give others. None of us are perfect. We can all be better humans daily. I also know there is still work to do on this healing journey. I hope that my story translates, that anything is possible. There are no battles you cannot face and win. There are no losses in life, only lessons. The things you have been through do not define who you are. How you fight back does, and how you win does. Moments of adversity will come; when they do, you do not let it stop you. The only thing constant is change. If we do not change, we do not grow. Give yourself grace in those seasons where you are not your best self because we all will have them. I hope that on your healing journey, you find yourself and love yourself unconditionally.

Thank you for taking the time to read this book and go on this first phase of my life with me. As previously stated, the story is still being written, and the journey is still being traveled.

I HOPE YOUR SPIRIT SOARS BEAUTIFUL SOULS.

LOVE,

BONITA RENEA

IF YOU KEEP READING… JUST A LITTLE BIT LONGER, I WROTE SOME POEMS REFLECTIVE OF THE STORY.

I CALL THIS NEXT PART **A WHOLE LOT OF NOTHING ABOUT SOMETHING**. SOME THINGS ARE MY STORY, SOME THINGS ARE THE STORIES OF THOSE I HAVE LOVED, AND SOME ARE THE STORIES OF ALL OF US. I HOPE WE ALL CAN TAKE WHAT WE NEED.

808'S AND HEARTBREAKS

They take our innocence and laugh at our cookouts. —family predator

Short Story
I will never forget the way his breath felt on my neck. The heavy panting and how wet my neck felt. I yelled, "Ouch!" He grabbed my neck and told me to "shut up." So I did. I was seven when he stripped my childhood away. And yet still, somehow, I felt this was all my fault. Down to the blood that flowed like a river in the tub.—Not a kid anymore

He set me free with the truth, but the lie…
    It tasted so much sweeter; it was tenderer, more free. So next time, baby, just lie to me.

This mediocre love has required me to dig into the deepest parts of my soul and love you with no conditions. And yet, you couldn't meet me halfway. What a shame that the love of my life couldn't just love me back. How insane, my love, that you could not love me as if you used to… Shit, or love me at all.

"I forgot how beautiful you are when you are happy."

Dear dad,
You ain't shit but a bunch of empty promises and some snacks to keep me quiet.

You're a liar, and it's crazy how you think I'm not gonna speak. "Baby girl, be quiet" when in my soul there is a riot, now I'm free.

All the women and the lies, she cried out to you. She wanted you more than anything; she wanted you to love her and be the man she needed, but instead, you broke her every day.

You lied to us; you told us you would change, and she believed you, but not me.

I knew you were a coward; that's why you hit on Queens, cause you needed power, you needed to boost your own self-esteem, cause you're a BITCH dad, you're not a man; all you did was lie.

If you couldn't have her, no one could; how could you be so selfish? Why didn't you ever think of me? You have other kids, too. You must love them way more than you love me because you let them keep their moms and took mine. I know you think you won, but you didn't, and I hope it haunts you forever.

I hope you see her smile and you cry. I hope the memory of her voice brings you pain. I hope your soul aches like mine did every day. It was some days I could not breathe.

And when the dust settles, I hope you say her name, scream out, and fall to your knees. Ask The Higher Being to forgive you for taking the life of a Queen, for killing a soul that bloomed so freely, and for taking her from her family. FOR TAKING HER FROM ME.

DEAR DAD,
YOU AINT SHIT BUT A BUNCH OF EMPTY PROMISES AND SOME SNACKS TO KEEP ME QUIET.

You broke me.
I broke me.
We broke me.
WE. BROKE.
—the blame game

You only loved me a little more than lonely,
Only a little more than a cold night, just a pinch more
Than an empty house, or a warm bed on one side.

If this is what love feels like, pain must be beautiful. I'll take more pain with a side of heartbreak, and if you want to show me how good it gets… Break me more; I'm built for this.

I'm wondering if tragic storms are how we water our grass
and the sunshine is just an illusion that we really do not need. AT ALL.
—SUNBURN

"You've warped me into you; now you don't want me.
—oh, the irony

You have taken things from me that I have only given to you.
I would ask for them back, but you gave them to her.

Short Story

You look at me with passion. There is nothing else that matters. At this moment, it is just you and me. We seem to fall for each other over and over.

And I can't stop looking into your eyes. She walks and stands next to you, and you look away… "DAMN."

Suddenly, the pain became a normal reality. I might live here forever.

Loving you, feels like
Walking on shattered glass
After it breaks. The glass feels better.

I'm your favorite toy when it is time to play. You pick me up gently, and it is not that often, but when you do, baby, we make magic. We make fire. I'd ask that next time you're done, don't throw me down so hard; it breaks me a little more each time. —TOY'S DEMISE

I looked at you, and you smiled.
The most beautiful smile I had seen in a while.
That was the moment I knew I was in love alone, and If
I stayed here; I'd always be.
—the reality

If waiting for you to love me right
Meant saving my life, don't bury me in a grave.
Take my ashes and throw them into the ocean so that I can just be.
SET ME FREE.

I've loved him more than I've loved myself; now he lives, and I wilt.
—what kind of flower is this?

All I have ever done is tell you how great you are and how great you look. All I have ever done is tell you why you are so amazing. And all you have asked is me to tell you more.
—Ungrateful Nigga

You keep telling me you will protect me, but
Who will protect me from you? In this broken-ass house,
With these walls painted in lies.
The air stinks. It smells like you and all of your stenches; they
roam in the air after you come home late.
Not even washing that dirty dick,
thinking you about to get some MORE pussy,
YOU AINT.

Either we really love each other, or we really hate each other. But the lines have to stay blurred, you see.

I'm scared to lose you, even though you have never belonged to me.

He loves the taste of my nectar.
He would drink me dry. But he
only seems to drink from my well when
He's not drifting, drinking the nectars of you.
—the other woman

> Everything in me knows
> You will never truly be mine.
> But this middling moment,
> It works just fine.

> He squeezed the life out of me
> And expected me to float. Funny
> How he believed I actually could.
> —drowning

> I have often wondered,
> Are we really in love? Or has
> Time made us comfortable enough
> In this bed of lies, to never get up.

The fire we shared came from
The bridges we burned, and the matches
We sparked when we torched this house;
We never made a home.

                Most days, I do not want to get out of bed.
           I'm hurting inside. I know I am alive, but I feel dead.
                            I'm tripping.
I know he is still thinking about me, too; I don't give a damn what he
      said. I'm about to text him, "Well damn, he left me on read".
                         —pit of delusion

His heart was cold, but his arms were warm when he held me.
I'll just stay here.

I'm not used to not having what I want. You are making
Me work for a love that does not exist, and for all the
Lies and shame. Now I am cold and alone on this floor,
Trying to catch my breath. Tears dried up because they
Don't even fall anymore. I am tired. If I just lay here,
I might die. And today, death feels easier than this.

How did you know I was lying?
Because you are a liar too.
You call me out on all my shit,
But what about you?
What about all my secrets you told,
From all the memories we shared. Or
All the times you acted like you gave a fuck,
But you never cared. Or what about the times,
I let you cry on my shoulder. And how we laughed and joked about how we would act when we got older. You really weren't shit for real, but maybe one day, we'll come back together when we both heal. Cause you had trauma, too, and you didn't know it, you tried to have a lot of pride, but in time, you folded. And maybe we'll be friends again, but we probably won't. I should wish your ass to hell, but hell is here on earth until we grow up a little more; here's to the rebirth.
—sike… girl fuck you…
—ok, sike again. It's all love. (Friendship heartbreaks hurt)

I did not feel beautiful or loved.
I felt drained and empty. I've never
Been alive here, but the days keep passing
And I keep letting them.

I have confused our passion with love. This lust takes over me, and I am taken by it. I know you are only here for my body because my mind is too potent, too raw, and too real. That's not what we do here, we do not feel. But you don't want to talk anyway; you want me to fuck you, so I will. You don't care to see inside my wounds, but you want to be in my womb. You know damn well you wouldn't put a baby there. See, I'm not that kind of woman to you. I'm not the one you take home. I'm the one that feeds every desire you crave, every fantasy you can taste, but not enough to love. I'm the one that only looks good in the dark.
—night light

My flowers can't bloom, no water
Runs from my well. The soul I had,
Has flown away. The life I live is a
Mere state of existence. I can't really see
Beyond your eyes, they have trapped me in
A wanderlust to get to wherever you are.
And now that I am where you are,
I really wish that I could be where I belong.
NOT HERE.

He lied. And not
The mean kind of lie.
It's not the kind of lie
that you can see
coming a mile away.
It was the kind of lie
That I fell in love with.
The lie that kissed my forehead
Ever so gently. The beautiful lie.
Yeah, that one.

ONE IS THE LONELIEST NUMBER

"Peace found me at
the side of death; peace won".

You have unlocked your magic black girl; you're
ready now. Tap into your power, black girl; I'll
show you how. See, you have been chosen black girl
Come and take your bow. No more running, no more
Hiding, take to the vow. To love who you are, black girl,
And to know your worth. To know what means something and to
let go of what hurts. To honor yourself and shine like the brightest Star.
You left yourself for a minute, but you did not go far. It's time, black girl,
you no longer have to fight; stand tall in your
magic, black girl; it's time to turn on your light.

I just walked back into myself, lifted my head up
A little bit and realized. Everything I am, I already was.

I just want to laugh,
smile, and be constantly flirty
and cute. I don't want to remember
the girl who used to laugh, I want to be her.
So today, I am going to be the girl that laughs,
A LOT.

I am not waiting for love to walk through
the door, I am waiting for me to.
—coming home

                              I'm me.
                        Crazy as hell,
                           Oh well.
                            I'm me.

I'm starting to think
That the moon can save
My spirit and I become
More like the stars that
Shine while we sleep.

I have Honey in my soul,
Magic in my veins, and fire in my blood.
I'm the daughter of love and the
Mother of light.
To get to me, you would have to
Kiss the sun and turn it into the
Moon…

The light from her aura makes flowers dance, even in the rain.

When hearts break, they do this little
dance as they come back together and heal.

I'm in these shadows, trying to figure out why this pain won't go away. Why can't the darkness turn to light, and I can see myself again? Am I dead? Is this what death looks like on the living? All this pain and trauma keeps forcing me to choose between the life I've always known and the life I want to create. Am I forcing this on myself, or is It really time for me to grow? Is it my time to become the being that I think I am, or am I the being that is becoming? Am I the sign that I have been waiting for?
—Questions Answered

She let chaos flood her village,
Now all that remains are ruins she's rebuilding. But this
Time with bricks of the highest vibration
And the soiled dirt from Mother Nature's womb.

You have given so much of
Your love away. Maybe
You should stash some,
Where the magic lies.
In that deep dark pit
Of your soul, because
The love you give requires
You, to love you, FIRST.

I'm learning how to be all the girls.
All the girls that I want to be and already am.
The fun girls with substance, the woke girls with style.
The smart girls with humor that will laugh until they cry.
The girls that don't mind dancing alone, or in a crowd.
The girls that make you wonder, "Why her"? The girls that
Make you feel something, even though, you do not quite
Know what it is. The girls that are sexy but still exude a Queen. The ones who have a smart mouth but are kind at the same time. I'm learning how to embrace the girls that are already me.

Look at you!
Glowing so effortlessly. Just like the moon.

We have to stop
Pretending to be
What we ain't. I ain't
Her, and this ain't it.
—CAP

> I decided to start
> actually healing
> these Wounds that
> I thought Just
> healed
> themselves. They
> still hurt.

Does everything you write about,
Have to be about Heartbreak?
—yes and no

This time, I choose me.
I have to choose me.
How can I not choose me?
Am I really choosing me? This time?
I am. This time. I am.
—pick a side, stay there

I visited the stars tonight and danced across the moon. I needed to be there to grow, to learn, to fly. It's high up there; I almost touched God's feet. I fell off for a second, but somehow, I was still very high. How? I started looking around, searching for her, for God. She tapped me on my shoulder and pointed to my heart. Then I knew she was there. Living inside of me, she had been there all along.

GEMS

Ever wanted something so badly that you gave it a little more than it deserved? Sacrificing what you want for someone who was not willing to make the sacrifice? There is a greater coming, DO NOT GIVE UP.

When someone wants you,
They will do whatever it takes to
Have you. If you have to question it,
Here is your answer.

There is this moment of clarity,
When a person realizes their worth.
Don't be on the side of no longer being worth it.

I think one of humans' most significant mistakes is allowing someone to decide who to like and dislike. We get caught up in what other people think, and we miss our own experiences. There are women who I have disliked or even fought. All based on another person's interpretation of them. We matured and realized our issue was not with each other; it was a mutual party. Life is really too short. Choose your own experience. Do not base it solely on another person because if you do, you are living someone else's truth; live your own.

The cosmic connection between
Two Beautiful Souls Vibing is a masterpiece
You're watching unfold. How amazing it is,
To create art in the form of love.

Why do we reopen toxic wounds and
call it seeking closure? Nothing has changed.
Please don't do it.

Know your worth.
There's a lot of them,
There's one you. Show them
Why you are the ONE.

Don't give so much of yourself that
You lose who you are in the process.
If they only bring half to the table, take
The table. Invest where it pours back into you. A blank deposit never clears.
—100% or nothing at all

Please do not give me my flowers when I die. I am here, a vessel, a person right now. When we transition into the next phase, the things we have said and done here will stay here. So ask yourself. "What kind of legacy am I leaving behind?" We are only here for a limited time to get it right with people. Please don't wait until a person dies to give them their flowers. You can right here, right now. Love is always love.

When you have it, you just have it.
The vibes, the aura, the light. It is a gift.
It can't be taught or duplicated.
Flow with that, and grow with that.

When something doesn't feel or seem right, follow your
Gut. It's whispers from The Higher Being shielding you from
a storm. Don't let it brew.

You did not break it; stop trying to fix it. Put it down. Now, pick you up.

> The sun, moon, and stars
> Have shown me God's beauty.
> Especially when they shine on me.

> Freeing myself from the things
> That held me captive.
> Feelings of doubt and uncertainty
> Can't be housed here.
> —brick house

I like her. I like
How she smiles when
She's happy. She really
Lights up the room, even
If it's empty. You can tell
She likes her too.

        The only moment that matters is right now.
        This very second. Both the past and
        The future is an illusion. So take care of
        Your spirit, your heart, and soul, RIGHT NOW. TODAY.

Two things can be true at once.
When it comes to deciding
Between who you used to be and who
You are meant to be, a separation must occur.
This will allow you to see exactly who you are and how you are built.
Pick your true.

There will be moments where
The load seems too heavy.
You may even want to quit or
Give up. This is a defining moment
For change. This moment defines
How you land. So fly. Even with
The extra weight strengthen
Those wings and soar.

Falling in love with
You may be your
Most extraordinary love story yet.
So, tell the story. And make
Sure, it sticks. It's yours.

Let things flow.
What's yours will not have to
Be chased. Everything is as it
Should be. Even the flow.

The sun and the stars.
The water and the earth.
The fire and the wind.
We need them all to blend.
This gift of life. To set us free
From all the trauma of the world.
Use them. God gave them to us.

Over here, we feel shit.
We feel it all. The good,
The bad, the indifferent.
When it hurts, we don't run,
We face it. Our feelings let
Us know that we are alive, that we are here.
So yeah, over here, we gon feel all of it, all the time.

Nobody is perfect. Find you somebody that loves you through all of your moments. The good, the bad, and the awful. Loving you through the good is easy, but someone who loves you in your ugly moments is imperative. Relationships are hard work. Make sure you are not basing what you want on what you see. Most people don't show the bad parts. Be your own goals. You should want something organic to YOU. Do not compare your story to someone else's. You never know what someone else is going through. It's your life. Don't get so caught up in watching someone else live, that you forget to.

>
> Everything is simply ok.
> It's ok to feel things.
> It's ok to want more.
> It's ok to "not feel like it".
> It's ok to laugh, laughter heals.
> It's ok to cry, crying cleanses.
> It's ok to be yourself.
> Billions of them. One YOU.
> Everything is simply ok.

www.ingramcontent.com/pod-product-compliance
Lightning Source LLC
LaVergne TN
LVHW012030060526
838201LV00061B/4544